MW00938908

Beginner ESL Lesson Plans for English Tutors: Section 1

Zhanna Hamilton

Table of Contents

Introduction:

Any freelance English as a second language tutor will tell you, tutoring can sometimes be challenge. It can be difficult to come up with lesson plans day in and day out for every student. That is why **Inspired By English** offers this guide for ESL tutors. Designed specifically with the freelance English tutor in mind, this guide provides 20 different lesson plans for beginner English learners.

Packed with lesson plans, tutoring tips, examples and even homework assignments – this lesson plan guide is all you will need for the first 20 sessions with each student. The great part about investing in an ESL lesson plan guide is that it pays for itself after just one or two lessons with one of your clients.

You can continually use it with every new beginner student, while confidently knowing they will get the speaking, listening, reading and writing practice they need. The lessons can be tailored to fit your students' specific needs - which means they will always be receiving the best possible individualized language instruction.

Languages help connect us to one another. If you have ever tried to learn a foreign language, you already know the struggles that come along with trying to learn everything at once. This guide allows you to break down the English language so that your students get a little bit of everything in manageable doses. Since overwhelming or dry lessons can be discouraging, this ESL lesson plan guide mixes different assignments and topics together to give you and your student more than one kind of tutoring session.

An English tutor often has a huge impact on their students, sometimes more than they know. Feel free to experiment with these lessons and change them according to your teaching style. Whether you are a budding English tutor or have been tutoring ESL for many years, these ESL lessons will make your line of work a lot easier. Houses are built following a blueprint, and your lessons should also have their own blueprint in order to produce the best possible results.

This language instruction series will continue to serve the private English tutor by releasing more beginner, intermediate and advanced ESL lesson plans. Check major retailers frequently for new releases from **Inspired By English**. These guides are designed to give you, the English tutor, more time to focus on inspiring your students and less time developing time-consuming lesson plans.

If you or your students need more English resources, you can find more at InspiredByEnglish.com. If you would like a free bonus gift for this purchase, find out how at the end of this guide. Thank you for teaching English to the world's English learners so that we can all communicate better and connect with each other.

ESL Lesson Plan 1: Asking Questions

Description: This lesson plan focuses on empowering the student to form simple questions. Asking questions will allow the student to get comfortable with speaking and English pronunciation, which is a common problem area among English learners. It will also allow them to ask questions they might have in real circumstances, giving them the confidence to inquire about issues in English when needed in their personal life.

Lesson Guide:

-Review "question words" with your student. Make sure they know the following words and how or when to use them:
-Who
-What
-When
-Where
-Which
-Why
-How

-Go over basic question formation. Practice with present simple structure. Make sure the student knows the basic question format:

question word + auxiliary verb + subject + main verb = simple present question

-Show the student examples of how to form simple present tense questions.

Examples:

Who does it bother?
What does Amy need?
When do you eat?
Where does John live?
Which do you prefer?
Why does she snore?
How does he sleep?

-Go over any new vocabulary within the questions that the student does not know.
-Have the student write out their own questions and then read them to you.
-Assign suggested homework for more simple tense question practice.

ESL Tutoring Tip: Advise your student to keep a notebook that is designated just for English notes. It should be small enough to carry around with them everywhere they go. This way, if they come across a billboard with an unknown phrase or a conversation that leaves them baffled, they can jot down the phrase or terms and research them later. This notebook will also be a great review for them of all the new vocabulary they are incorporating on a daily basis. The notebook can also be electronic if the student carries a smart phone or a PC tablet everywhere.

Homework: Asking Questions

Circle the correct **question word** and **auxiliary verb**. It is possible for more than one **question word** to be grammatically correct. Each **question word** changes the meaning of the question being asked. Make sure you understand the differences between the questions.

1. (Where/What) (do/does) Sally want?

2. (Where/Which) (do/does) Ashley live?

3. (Who/What) (do/does) Peter date?

4. (Which/Where) (do/does) Mary like?

5. (Who/How) (do/does) it eat?

6. (Who/Where) (do/does) you sleep?

7. (Why/Who) (do/does) you work?

8. (Where/Who) (do/does) Kevin love?

9. (Which/What) (do/does) you think?

10. (Where/Who) (do/does) Leah eat?

11. (How/Which) (do/does) she want?

12. (What/Where) (do/does) Peter stay?

13. (How/Who) (do/does) you drive?

14. (Where/What) (do/does) Kelly do?

15. (What/Where) (do/does) Mandy work?

16. (Where/Who) (do/does) you eat?

17. (Why/What) (do/does) you do?

18. (Why/What) (do/does) she like?

19. (Why/Who) (do/does) she draw?

20. (How/Which) (do/does) he want?

ESL Lesson Plan 2: Common Routines

Description: This lesson focuses on describing the daily routines of the student. It will allow them to practice forming sentences and describing their day. Both ordinary tasks and routines unique to the student should be taught.

Lesson Guide:

-Go over ordinary, everyday tasks that most people do in the morning, afternoon and evening.
-Explain how continuous, daily actions are described in the simple present tense.

Examples:

I wake up.
I go to the bathroom.
I brush my teeth.
I make coffee/tea.
I eat breakfast.
I drink coffee/tea.
I take a shower.
I get dressed.
I go to work.
I work.
I go to lunch.
I take a coffee/tea break.
I make small talk with my coworkers.
I go home.

I make dinner.
I eat dinner.
I watch television.
I browse the internet.
I spend time with my family.
I read a book.
I brush my teeth.
I wash my face.
I set my alarm clock.
I go to bed.

-Go over any new vocabulary within the sentences that the student does not know.
-Have the student write out their own sentences unique to their day.
-Have them describe their typical day, using their sentences as a reference.
-Assign suggested homework for more simple present tense sentence practice.

Homework: Common Routines

Write out 10 of your common activities in three different settings.

Examples of settings include:

-Gym
-Highway
-Supermarket
-Coffee Shop
-Mall
-Post Office
-Movie Theater
-Restaurant
-Kitchen
-Park
-Beach
-Bar
-Garden
-Living Room
-Patio/Balcony
-Friend's House

Example of 10 Common Activities at the Library:

1. I walk into the library.
2. I look for my favorite genre.
3. I browse the books in my favorite genre.
4. I take some books with me to a table.
5. I browse each book.

6. I put some books back.
7. I take the books I like to the librarian.
8. I check out the books I like.
9. I make small talk with the librarian.
10. I leave the library.

ESL Lesson Plan 3: Describing People's Physical Appearances

Description: This lesson gives the student the necessary vocabulary to describe a person's physical appearance. Common descriptions will be reviewed. The student will also learn how to describe themselves to others.

Lesson Guide:

-Go over common description words for physical appearances.
-Make sure to cover words for describing hair, eyes, skin, height and weight.
-Give the student the vocabulary to describe significant features as well, such as scars.

Examples:

Descriptions for Hair:

Long
Shoulder-length
Short

Curly
Wavy
Straight

Black

Blonde
Dirty Blonde
Brown
Red
Grey
White
Bald

Descriptions for Eyes:

Green
Blue
Brown
Grey

Descriptions for Skin:

Light-skinned
Tan
Dark-skinned

Descriptions for Height:

Short
Average Height
Tall
____ Feet and ____ Inches Tall

Descriptions for Weight/Body Type:

Skinny

Average Weight
Heavyset
Athletic Build
Obese

Descriptions for Significant Features:

Dimples
Cleft Lip
Cleft Chin
Scar
Wears Glasses
Wrinkles
Beard

-Mention any other possible options for describing someone's physical appearance, such as their **ethnicity**, **sex** or **age**.
-Have the student describe at least 3 different people or pictures of people.
-Assign the suggested homework for more practice on describing people's appearances.

ESL Tutoring Tip: Encourage your student to strike up a conversation with friendly-looking strangers. This will be a scary task for them at first, but they will soon find that speaking to strangers is not that difficult. It will allow them to practice their English and to practice their listening skills.

Your student will probably fear not being understood, which is natural. To overcome this fear, you can rehearse what they want to say to a stranger during a lesson. The conversation can be as short as a greeting or as long as asking for directions.

Allow the student to decide what is most comfortable for them and congratulate them even for the smallest of accomplishments (even small accomplishments take a lot of courage when conversing in a foreign language).

Homework: Describing People's Physical Appearances

Describe the physical characteristics of the people below.
Write out full sentences and read them out loud.

Example Description Sentences:

The woman has long hair.
The man has dimples.

Your turn!

21

ESL Lesson Plan 4: Small Talk

Description: This lesson will allow the student to practice small talk so that they will be more comfortable when talking to strangers. Small talk is especially important for English learners, as it gives them something to talk about with native English speakers. Perfecting this skill can boost their confidence when speaking English.

Lesson Guide:

-Define small talk to your student and give examples of how it is used.
-Provide the vocabulary necessary for chatting with a stranger or associate.

Topic Examples:

-The Weather
-Traffic
-A Long Line
-Greetings

-Role-play with your student from a script. Once they are comfortable making small talk, practice conversing without a script.
-Incorporate small talk into each lesson by initiating it at the beginning of every lesson. This will allow your student to get used to chatting and will make it easier

for them to initiate themselves with a stranger or associate.

Example Scripts:

Talking about the Weather at work:

Person 1: "Nice weather we are having today, don't you think?"
Person 2: "Yes, I love sunny days."
Person 1: "Me too! It puts me in a good mood."
Person 2: "Same here. But, it makes me a little lazy, too."
Person 1: "Oh, I get that way, too. It's hard not to think of the beach while you're at work when the weather is so perfect!"

Talking about Traffic at Work:

Person 1: "The traffic on the way to work was terrible!"
Person 2: "I know, rush hour in the morning is always bad in this area."
Person 1: "Oh well, at least we made it on time."
Person 2: "Right! That's a good attitude."
Person 1: "Thanks! Alright, talk to you later."
Person 2: "Ok, see you."

Talking about the Long Line While Waiting in Line:

Person 1: "Wow, this line is never-ending! Good thing I don't have plans within the next five minutes."
Person 2: "Right? I feel like we've been standing here for hours."
Person 1: "It might be because it's lunch time for everyone. Next time I'll remember to come at a different time."
Person 2: "That's a good idea. I think I'll do the same."

Greeting a Colleague at Work:

Person 1: "Good morning! How was your commute?"
Person 2: "It was not bad, surprisingly. How about yours?"
Person 1: "It was pretty smooth, too. I hope it's like that all week."
Person 2: "Wouldn't that be nice!"
Person 1: "It certainly would be."

-Practice the suggested scripts, or make your own that are more unique to your student.
-Make sure your student looks at you when speaking and not down at the paper. This will help them with eye contact and facial cues.
-Assign the suggested homework assignment.
-Be prepared to correct and practice your student's scripts.

Homework: Small Talk

Think of three different scenarios in your everyday life where you would need to make small talk.
Write out exactly what is usually said.
Have your tutor check for grammatical errors during your next lesson.
Practice the scripts you've created with your tutor.

ESL Lesson Plan 5: Phrasal Verbs

Description: Since phrasal verbs are an essential part of the English language, it is a good idea for your student to begin learning them. Phrasal verbs will help your student combine words more efficiently and learn the common patterns of word combinations.

Lesson Guide:

-Go over some common phrasal verbs with your student.
-Make sure they know if a phrasal verb has more than one meaning.
-Make sure they understand which phrasal verbs are separable and which ones are not.
-You will not be able to teach them every single phrasal verb in one lesson, so focus only on commonly used phrasal verbs.

Examples:
Inseparable Phrasal Verbs:

Ask for
Back out
Catch up
Come across
Drop in
Hold on
Look after
Run away

Stick to
Take off

Separable Phrasal Verbs:

Add up
Bring up
Calm down
Cheer up
Give back
Move over
Pass up
Pick up
Stand up
Think over

-Give them the definition of each phrasal verb, along with examples on how to use them.
-If you need more phrasal verb information, Inspired By English has published a guide called "The Best Phrasal Verbs and How to Use Them" which is available at Amazon, iTunes, Barnes and Noble and all other major retailers. It is offered as a paperback, ebook and audio book.
-Assign the suggested homework and be prepared to check your student's work during the next lesson.

Homework: Phrasal Verbs

Fill in the correct phrasal verb from the word bank for each sentence. Some phrasal verbs may be used more than once, and some may not be used at all. The phrasal verbs may be in any tense. Examine the sentences and determine the best phrasal verb for each statement.

Word Bank:

Ask for	Add up
Back out	Bring up
Catch up	Calm down
Come across	Cheer up
Drop in	Give back
Hold on	Move over
Look after	Pass up
Run away	Pick up
Stick to	Stand up
Take off	Think over

1. Jamie _____ her little brother while her mother went to the store.

2. Samantha _____ on her grandmother to make sure she was doing okay.

3. Kevin tried to _____ his little sister _____ after her toy broke.

4. "_____ your candy _____ to your mother; you are not allowed to eat

sweets before dinner." said Mandy's grandmother.

5. I _____ a giant seashell while I was walking along the beach today.

6. Peter _____ of the deal last minute. He didn't think it was worth it.

7. Sally needed to _____ before she could confront her boss about her lowered salary. She felt too angry to speak.

8. "You need to _____ after yourself. The house is a mess." scolded Kevin's mother.

9. Jamie needed to _____ the couch _____ to make room for her new ottoman.

10. "_____ it _____ before you say no. You can let me know your decision tomorrow." said Ashley, after offering Mandy a job.

11. Alice _____ a stray cat by her house and decided she would feed it every day.

12. "Can you _____ me _____ at 8 p.m.?" asked Tina.

13. "I haven't seen you in years! Let's get coffee together and _____." said Yolanda to her old friend from high school.

14. "After hurting my ankle while running, I decided I'll _____ walking." joked Anandra.

15. John hurt his foot right before the camping trip and needed to _____ at the last minute.

16. "I've been sitting for so long, I need to _____ for a few minutes and walk around." said John.

17. "I don't want to _____ this opportunity _____, but I have already made plans for that day." said Amy when she realized her company's holiday party was on the same day as her sister's birthday.

18. "Will you _____ my son for five minutes? I need to go to the bathroom." asked Mandy.

19. "I tried to pet the stray dog, but he _____ from me.' said Ricky.

20. "Please _____ your shoes before entering the house. You can walk around barefoot inside." requested Martha.

ESL Lesson Plan 6: Simple Future Tense

Description: Students must be able to comfortably explain future events and should have a good understanding of the simple future tense grammatical structures. In this lesson, they will learn the basic simple future formats and will have a chance to practice creating future tense sentences. It is also vital to spend enough time allowing the student to practice speaking in the future tense, so that it will be easier for them to do so in between lessons.

Lesson Guide:

-Introduce the student to some common simple future sentence structures.
-Form future tense sentences together on paper and have the student read them out loud.

Examples of Simple Future Tense Sentence Structures:

Subject + **Going to** + Verb

Subject + **Will** + Verb

Examples of Simple Future Tense Sentences:

I will go to the store.

She will need more clothing.

He will not want more food.

Peter will speak at the conference.

Mandy will walk to her car.

I am going to go home.

She is going to eat at 6 p.m.

He is going to drive his car.

Kevin is going to buy more cat food.

Ashley is going to visit her friend.

-Make sure the student is comfortable with creating and saying their own future tense sentences.
-Assign the suggested homework and be prepared to correct during your next lesson.

ESL Tutoring Tip: If your student has a difficult time with pronouncing certain sounds, carry a small mirror with you and have them imitate your mouth movements while directly watching their own mouths with the mirror you provide.

Just as a dancer watches their dance moves through a mirror, so should a student first learning to imitate a native English speaker. This will also help them realize any continuous mistakes they are making with their mouths that are preventing them from pronouncing words correctly.

Homework: Simple Future Tense

Part 1: Think of your day tomorrow. Write out 20 simple future tense sentences about your day tomorrow and what you are going to do.

Part 2: Select the correct simple future tense for each sentence.

1. Sally is (going to/will) the party tonight.

2. He (going to/will) need a ride home.

3. She is (going to/will) bake cookies over the weekend.

4. Leah is (going to/will) come over to Brandy's house this Friday.

5. Peter (going to/will) not babysit his sister's children because he has no experience with children.

6. Kevin (going to/will) going on a camping trip this weekend.

7. Mary is (going to/will) find out who stole her bicycle.

8. Jane (going to/will) need to buy the ingredients for her new recipe.

9. I am (going to/will) come with you to France.

10. Peter (going to/will) get is haircut tomorrow.

11. Martha is (going to/will) be late for the party.

12. Susan (going to/will) not be joining us tonight.

13. Madison (going to/will) leave for Italy in the morning.

14. He is (going to/will) buy medicine for his sore throat.

15. She is (going to/will) visit her grandmother soon.

16. The company is (going to/will) donate more money to charity this year.

17. Kevin is (going to/will) buy new sneakers.

18. Jake (going to/will) not wash the dishes if there are too many of them.

19. Peter (going to/will) take his children to school this week.

20. Mandy is (going to/will) clean her home on Sunday.

ESL Lesson Plan 7: Emotions

Description: Students need to know how to describe the emotional states of others as well as themselves. This lesson will teach them the basic vocabulary for describing common emotional states. The student will also get the opportunity to speak about their own emotions.

Lesson Guide:

-List and explain the most common emotions.
-Show the student a simple sentence structure for describing their and others' emotional states.

Examples of Common Emotions:

-Happy
-Sad
-Excited
-Angry
-Jealous
-Energetic
-Anxious
-Determined
-Annoyed
-Relaxed
-Nervous
-Confident
-Playful
-Grateful

-Proud
-Tired
-Focused
-Enthusiastic
-In Love
-Surprised

Examples of Simple Sentence Structures for Emotions:

Subject + am/is/are + emotion

Subject + feel/feels + emotion

-Now that the student has the vocabulary and the sentence structures, they can start forming their own sentences.
-Have the student write down 10 different sentences with emotional states.
-Have the student read their sentences out loud.
-Ask the student to describe their own emotional state that day in full sentences.
-Ask your student if there is a particular emotional state that they want to know the vocabulary for that has not previously been mentioned.
-Assign the suggested homework and be prepared to correct it during your next tutoring session with them.

Homework: Emotions

Write a short children's story about a fictional character. The story should be between 200-400 words. Explain what happens to your character and how they feel about it. Use as many emotions as possible. Don't worry about creating a unique and exciting story (although, that will be more fun for your English tutor to read). Instead, focus on correctly using vocabulary for emotions.

ESL Lesson Plan 8: Greetings

Description: Students need to know the different ways to greet their friends, family, colleagues and strangers. With this lesson, you will equip them with the proper greeting for every person in their life. The student will need to understand the informal and formal ways of greeting someone and when it is appropriate.

Lesson Guide:

-Ask the student the types of greetings they are already familiar with and list those as either formal or informal on a piece of paper. Explain the best places or ways to use those greetings.
-Make a list with the student of more formal and informal ways of greeting the people in their life.
-While creating the list, role-play with your student by practicing the various greetings with each other.
-Explain any phraseology that is unfamiliar to your student during your role-playing.

Examples of Formal and Informal Greetings:

Good morning.
Good afternoon.
Good evening.
How's it going?
Hello.
Hi.
Hey.

What's up?
How ya' doin'?
Sup?

-Make sure the student understands that not all greetings (especially informal ones) are necessary to incorporate into their own vocabulary for actual use. Instead, teach it to them so that they are familiar with the terminology when presented with it outside of tutoring.
-Share your favorite informal and formal greetings with your student.
-Cover some of the common responses they should expect to receive when using certain greetings.
-Assign the suggested homework and remember to ask your student about it during your next tutoring session with them.

Homework: Greetings

Incorporate any useful formal or informal greetings into your everyday life by using them on your friends, family, colleagues and strangers. This is especially helpful if the person you are speaking to is a native English speaker. Listen closely for their natural responses. Later, write them down and discuss your overall responses to your new vocabulary with your tutor.

ESL Lesson Plan 9: Conversation about Pets

Description: English learners need to know how to have conversations about common subjects. One common subject in the United States is pets (mainly cats and dogs). In this lesson, your student will learn the vocabulary and sentence structures necessary to talk about their and other people's pets.

Lesson Guide:

-Ask your student if they have any pets or about their experience with animals in their native country.
-Introduce the student to basic vocabulary and sentences that will allow them to have a conversation about animals or pets.

Example Vocabulary for Discussing Pets:

Kitten(s)
Cat(s)
Puppy/Puppies
Dog(s)
Leash
Litter Box
Food Bowl
Water Bowl
Collar(s)
Veterinarian
Fleas
Play Fetch

Purr
Meow
Hiss
Bark
Growl
Pet (verb)
Dry Pet Food
Wet Pet Food
Catnip
Chew Toy(s)
Whiskers
Tail(s)
Paw(s)

Example Sentence Structures:

I own a (type of animal).

I have a (type of animal).

I used to have a (type of animal).

Your (type of animal) is so cute!

I want to get a (type of animal).

Do you have any pets?

How many pets do you have?

I don't have any pets.

I have (number) pet(s).

I love (type of animal; i.e. cats, dogs, etc.).

What kind of (type of animal) do you have?

I have a (breed of animal).

-Have your student read these and other relevant statements out loud.
-Correct any pronunciation mistakes and let your student know they can take their time pronouncing difficult sounds at first.
-Practice having a conversation about pets with your student as many times as necessary. By the end of the lesson, he or she should feel comfortable discussing their pet or their opinions about pets.
-Assign the suggested homework and remember to ask about it during your next tutoring session.

Homework: Conversation about Pets

Strike up a conversation with a friend or colleague about pets. If you are feeling bold, comment on a dog being walked by a stranger and have a conversation with them about pets. During the conversation, practice the terminology you learned during your lesson. Pay attention to what and how the other person says and write it down after the conversation is over for reference. This exercise is most helpful is the other person is a native English speaker.

ESL Lesson Plan 10: Speaking in Simple Past Tense (Regular Verbs)

Description: Many conversations in English revolve around discussing past events and what we have done. During this lesson, your student will review simple past tense usage. They will also have the opportunity to practice a conversation in the past tense with you, as speaking is one of the hardest aspects of the English language for many English learners. This practice will help the student become aware of their tense usage and to adjust it accordingly when conversing in English.

Lesson Guide:

-Review simple past tense usage with the student. Make sure they understand it is used when an action was performed in the past and is no longer being performed.
-Stick to explain regular verbs and devote another lesson completely to irregular verbs.
-Review some common verbs that have a simple past tense ending in –ed.

Examples of Simple Past Tense Regular Verbs:

Walk = Walked
Live = Lived
Wait = Waited
Play = Played
Work = Worked

Listen = Listened
Travel = Traveled
Visit = Visited
Discover = Discovered
Like = Liked
Love = Loved
Brush = Brushed
Exercise = Exercised
Talk = Talked
Look = Looked
Clean = Cleaned
Need = Needed
Miss = Missed
Waste = Wasted
Cook = Cooked
Wash = Washed
Laugh = Laughed
Smile = Smiled
Kiss = Kissed
Attend = Attended
Miss = Missed
Borrow = Borrowed

-Have your student read the present and past tense versions of each regular verb.
-Teach them the correct way to pronounce each past tense, noting where the –ed ending has a "t" sound instead of a "d" sound.
-Create sentences together using the regular past tense verbs just learned and have your student say them out loud.

-Assign the suggested homework and remember to ask about it during your next tutoring session.

ESL Tutoring Tip: It takes many years to become fluent in English, and you need to let your student know that the path to sounding close to a native English speaker is a long one. There is no magic pill they can take that will make them fluent overnight.

They will make many mistakes, but each mistake teaches them a lesson and brings them closer to fluency. This is why they should not be afraid of making errors in their speech or anywhere else in the English language. Let your student know that it is not a question of whether they will make mistakes or not (because they will), but rather how fast they can learn from them and move towards a higher level of English.

Set mini milestones for your student and congratulate them when they correct their own errors or take initiative in bettering their fluency faster (i.e. asking for more homework assignments). The levels of ambition will vary from student to student depending on their life goals. As the tutor, you should do everything you can to encourage and inspire your student to strive for excellence.

Homework: Speaking in Simple Past Tense (Regular Verbs)

Watch your favorite movie and focus only on their usage of past tense regular verbs. How many can you hear? Write them down. You can use subtitles if you have a difficult time understanding spoken English. If you hear any new regular verbs that you do not know, highlight them after jotting them down. When the movie is over or when you are done listening for past tense regular verbs, look up the definitions for the newly learned verbs. How many new words did you learn? Try to incorporate them into your speech the next time you are speaking to a native English speaker. Also, share them with your English tutor during your next tutoring session.

ESL Lesson Plan 11: Speaking in Simple Past Tense (Irregular Verbs)

Description: English learners will not be able to survive knowing only regular verb tenses. They must also learn the strange conjugations of irregular verbs. In this lesson, they will get familiar with common irregular verbs and how to use them in their simple past tense forms.

Lesson Guide:

-Ask your student what irregular verbs they already know and write them down.
-Introduce your student to other common irregular verbs and show them how to spell the verbs in their simple past tenses.

Examples of Simple Past Tense Irregular Verbs:

Awake = Awoke

Dream = Dreamt/Dreamed

Eat = Ate

Speak = Spoke

Find = Found

Be = Was/Were

Drive = Drove

Let = Let

Spend = Spent

Understand = Understood

Take = Took

Sleep = Slept

Tell = Told

Begin = Began

Catch = Caught

Grow = Grew

Hang = Hung

Fly = Flew

Light = Lit

Freeze = Froze

Drink = Drank

Come = Came

Cut = Cut

Make = Made

Win = Won

Swim = Swam

Write = Wrote

Rise = Rose

Sell = Sold

Read = Read

Hit = Hit

Have = Had

Do = Did

-Read of each irregular verb and have your student read them out loud.

-Make sure to go over proper pronunciation of each irregular verb's simple past tense.

-Have your student create sentences for each new irregular verb they learned. The sentence should be in the simple past tense.

-Assign the suggested homework and remember to ask about it during your next tutoring session.

Homework: Speaking in Simple Past Tense (Irregular Verbs)

Write a short story using the irregular verbs you have learned during your lesson. The story should be at least 500 words and should be written in the simple past tense. Then, read the story a few times until you feel comfortable with it.

Once you are comfortable, read it one more time while recording your voice on a sound recorder of your choice (preferably a portable sound recorder). Play back your recording. Can you catch your mistakes in pronunciation? During your next tutoring session, play the recording for your tutor and have them correct your pronunciation.

If you do not have a sound recorder, you can still do this exercise by reading your story to yourself multiple times and then reading it again during your next lesson. Although, if you have not practiced reading the story in a while, you might have a harder time reading the story smoothly. To make it easier for yourself, practice reading it right before the lesson. That way, the pronunciation of each word will be fresh in your mind.

ESL Lesson Plan 12: Synonyms of Adjectives

Description: Synonyms are a great way to diversify the vocabulary of an English learner. They will allow a student to have more than one way of saying or writing their thoughts. This can make the language much more interesting for them, especially if they love to write. In this lesson, you will be teaching your student synonyms for common adjectives. On top of possibly learning new words, your student will also learn their most common synonyms.

Lesson Guide:

-Ask your student to list some of their favorite adjectives. Make sure they are pronouncing each one of them correctly. It is easier to correct a word's pronunciation early on in an English learner's education than it is to break years of bad speaking habits. Catch bad pronunciation early and help your student learn the proper way of saying common words.
-Begin a synonym list for each word. Each term should not have more than three common synonyms. This will make it easier for your student to memorize them and incorporate them into their own vocabulary.
-For every new word learned, allow your student to take their time learning its proper pronunciation.

Examples of Words and Their Synonyms:

Nice: Charming – Considerate – Kind

Brave: Adventurous – Fearless – Heroic

Beautiful: Gorgeous – Attractive – Good-Looking

Strong: Able-Bodied – Mighty – Tough

Eager: Ambitious – Antsy – Avid

Dangerous: Risky – Hazardous – Fatal

Angry: Enraged – Furious – Hateful

Generous: Giving – Charitable – Considerate

Tired: Exhausted – Sleepy – Fatigued

Inspired: Moved – Influenced – Excited

Excellent: Great – Outstanding – Wonderful

Strange: Abnormal – Unusual – Bizarre

Cute: Adorable – Delightful – Charming

Clean: Neat – Orderly – Tidy

-Have your student use each newly-learned word in a sentence spoken out loud and written down for future reference.

-Read of the original word one at a time and ask the student to say at least one of its reviewed synonyms.
-Assign the suggested homework and review it during your next tutoring session.

Homework: Synonyms of Adjectives

Make flashcards from your adjective notes.
Write the original adjective on one side and the three
synonyms on the other side.
Next, shuffle the cards and read off the first card.
Try to list the three synonyms by memory.
Create a sentence out loud for each synonym.
Do this for all of the flashcards.
Bring your flashcards to your next tutoring session.
Your tutor will pick random cards and ask you to recite
its synonyms.
Your tutor will also make sure your pronunciation is
improving
by correcting any errors in speech during this review.

ESL Lesson Plan 13: Antonyms of Adjectives

Description: Just as English learners need to know synonyms to have variety in their speech and writing, their knowledge of antonyms is equally important. In this lesson, the student will review words with opposite meanings. Some of these the student might already know, and some will be new to them. Regardless of whether or not they already know certain vocabulary, this is a great opportunity to correct any pronunciation or enunciation errors.

Lesson Guide:

-Ask the student which adjective antonyms they already know and have your student write them down.
-Create a list of other antonyms of common adjectives with them, noting their pronunciation along the way.

Examples of Antonyms for Common Adjectives:

Good – Bad

Nice – Mean

Pure – Impure

Big – Small

Generous – Greedy

Sweet – Sour

Strong – Weak

Bright – Dark

Smart – Stupid

Forgiving – Vengeful

Beautiful – Ugly

Happy – Sad

Obedient – Rebellious

Anxious – Relaxed

Wet – Dry

Light – Heavy

Clear – Blurry

Easy – Hard

Normal – Strange

Fast – Slow

Large – Small

-After introducing the list of antonyms to your student, read them off to him or her and have them give you each word's antonym.

-Assign the suggested homework and review it with your student during your next tutoring session.

Homework: Antonyms of Adjectives

-Make flashcards with the vocabulary learned from the lesson.

-On the back of each card, write the front word's corresponding antonym.

-Review each card, reciting the antonym from memory.

-Create a sentence out loud for every antonym new to your vocabulary.

-After you have gone through all of the cards once, try the same exercise backwards (reading the antonym and reciting opposing adjective from memory).

-During your next tutoring session, hand the flash cards over to your tutor.

-Your tutor will say either the antonym or the original word to you, and you can recite its corresponding word.

ESL Lesson Plan 14: Present Progressive Tense

Description: In this lesson, the student will learn about the present progressive (also known as the present continuous) tense. Whether this is a review or completely new to your student, it is important to make sure they know how to conjugate their verbs into this tense correctly.

Lesson Guide:

-Explain to your student when the present continuous tense is used. Let them know that this tense is for describing a continuous action in the present. It can also describe an ongoing action that did not recently start, but has not yet stopped.

-Show your student an example sentence format and some example sentences with this tense.

-Make sure your student already knows how to conjugate "to be". If not, teach them this step first, as they will need to know this in order to properly construct a sentence in the present progressive tense.

Example Sentence Format for the Present Progressive Tense:

to be + verb + -ing

Present Tense Conjugation of "to be":

I am

You are
She/He/It is
We are
You are
They are

Example Sentences:

I **am singing** in the rain.

He **is laughing** a lot today.

She **is cooking** right now.

Peter **is dancing** with Sally.

Jonathan **is enjoying** a glass of wine.

Amanda **is brushing** her teeth.

He **is checking** is email.

Kelly **is painting** a picture.

We **are sitting** in the middle of the floor.

They **are chatting** on the phone.

I **am making** coffee.

She **is giving** her baby a bath.

He **is laughing** at a funny joke.

-Have your student read the examples out loud.
-Let them create their own example sentences with this tense.
-Correct any pronunciation or enunciation errors.
-Assign the suggested homework and be prepared to correct it during your next tutoring session.

Homework: Present Progressive Tense

Fill in the correct "to be" conjugation.
Conjugate the main verb of each sentence into the present progressive tense.

1. Mary _____ (bake) cookies.

2. Jane _____ (pour) a glass of water.

3. He _____ (make) a lot of noise.

4. We _____ (watch) a movie.

5. They _____ (write) notes in their

notebooks.

6. She _____ (sing) a song.

7. Kevin _____ (carry) a large box.

8. Diane _____ (play) on her guitar.

9. George _____ (win) against Robin in

chess.

10. Alice _____ (pet) her cat.

11. Penny _____ (kiss) her boyfriend.

12. Leah _____ (listen) to music on her ipod.

13. He _____ (have) dinner with his friends.

14. We _____ (be) silly together.

15. I _____ (try) to make homemade bread.

16. We _____ (express) our feelings.

17. He _____ (study) for an important test.

18. I _____ (hold) my cat in my arms.

19. The lifeguard _____ (watch) the people in the water.

20. Jill _____ (grow) a garden in her backyard.

21. The little boy _____ (discover) new things every day.

22. The scientist _____ (experiment) with different methods.

23. The janitor _____ (sweep) the hallway in the school.

24. The teacher _____ (teach) the students math.

25. We _____ (listen) to the professor give a lecture on physics.

26. The mother _____ (worry) about her son who is not home yet.

27. The waitress _____ (take) someone's order.

28. The Marine _____ (serve) their country through active duty service.

29. The monkey _____ (climb) the tree at the zoo.

30. The college students _____ (discuss)

politics with one another.

ESL Lesson Plan 15: Conversation about Food

Description: A common conversation among people is one about food, which your student needs to know how to master. In this lesson, your student will learn how to express their opinions about food. They will expand their vocabulary and learn how to discuss not only the different type of food, but also the various states of hunger and the different types of diets common in the United States.

Lesson Guide:

-Your student may already know certain questions and vocabulary about food. Ask them to list what foods and phrases they already know. If they know a substantial amount, then jump right into teaching them without their list. You can adjust your lesson along the way according to your student's knowledge. It is still a good idea to go over any words or phrases that your student is already familiar with so that you may check for proper pronunciation and enunciation.

-Create a new list with your student on common phrases pertaining to food, common foods, the various types of diets and sentence formats for talking about food.

Examples of Common Food Statements:

Are you hungry?

I am (not) hungry.

I am starving!

What do you want to eat?

I would like to eat _____.

I lost my appetite.

I (don't) know what I want to eat.

I am (not) on a diet.

I (do not) eat meat.

I am (not) picky with my food.

What is your favorite (type of) food?

My (least) favorite food is _____.

What do you usually eat for

(breakfast/lunch/dinner)?

I am (not) thirsty.

What would you like to drink?

Are you thirsty?

What is your favorite beverage?

My (least) favorite beverage is _____.

I love to drink _____.

Examples of Diet Types:

-Paleo

-Vegetarian

-Vegan

-Low Carbohydrates

-Low Calorie

-Low Fat

-Belief-Based (i.e. no pork for religious reasons)

Examples of Common Food in the United States:

Vegetables:

-Carrots

-Lettuce

-Broccoli

-Onions

-Celery

-Zucchini

-Cucumbers

Fruits:

-Apples

-Bananas

-Pears

-Peaches

-Cherries

-Oranges

-Blueberries

Common Dishes:

-Meatballs and Pasta

-Pizza

-Lasagna

-Macaroni and Cheese

-Burger and Fries

-Sandwiches

-Salads

-Soups

-Review all terms and sentences with your student. Have your student recite each word or sentence. Pay close attention to their pronunciation and correct any errors.
-Role-play a conversation about food. You can try this multiple times and give different answers during each conversation in order to practice with a larger vocabulary.
-Assign the suggested homework and remember to ask about it during your next tutoring session.

Homework: Conversation about Food

During this homework assignment, you will be asking questions in English about food.
Recite the questions below to yourself a few times.
Get comfortable saying them out loud.
Find a native English speaker. This can be a classmate, a friend or even your tutor.
Ask them these questions and record their answers.
You do not have to record the answers in full sentences.
When you are finished, make full sentences out of your notes from your interview.

For example:

Your Question: "What is your favorite food?"
Their Answer: "Pasta."
You Write: Amy's favorite food is pasta.

What is your favorite (type of) food?

What is your favorite beverage?

What do you usually eat for breakfast?

What do you normally eat for lunch?

What do you typically eat for dinner?

Do you like dessert?

What is your (least) favorite type of dessert?

What is your favorite fruit?

What is your favorite vegetable?

Do you prefer coffee or tea (if any)?

Do you drink a lot of water?

How many meals per day do you normally eat?

Do you usually make dinner at home or do you eat out?

What is your favorite restaurant?

What is your favorite dish to cook at home?

ESL Lesson Plan 16: Conversation about People

Description: In this lesson, the English learner will practice speaking about other people. This practice will teach them to describe how they are related to other people, how they met their friends, how they know their acquaintances and how to introduce their friends or family to others. Since speaking is a problematic area for many English learners, take your time with the lesson. Correct any pronunciation and enunciation errors early, so that the student is aware of the correct way of conversing.

Lesson Guide:

-Your student might already know many terms for describing other people's relations to them. Ask them what they already know and write it down with them.
-Teach them additional terms and sentence formats that will give them the vocabulary to speak about their family, colleagues, or friends.
-Take your time and listen closely for errors. Make sure your student is learning the right way to say each word the first time. If they already have mistakes within their speech, now is the time to teach them the correct way of speaking.

Examples of Vocabulary Describing Relations to Others:

Related:

-Mother
-Father
-Brother
-Sister
-Aunt
-Uncle
-Cousin
-Niece
-Nephew
-Grandfather
-Grandmother
-Great Grandfather
-Great Grandmother
-Daughter
-Son
-Grandson
-Granddaughter

Not Related:

-Neighbor
-Friend
-Colleague
-Boss
-Acquaintance
-Classmate
-Boyfriend
-Girlfriend
-Fiancé
-Fiancée

-Wife
-Husband
-Son-in-Law
-Daughter-in-Law
-Mother-in-Law
-Father-in-Law

Example Sentence Structures for Describing Relations:

How are you two related?

He/she is my _____ (type of relation i.e.

brother/sister).

We are _____ (type of relation, i.e. cousins).

This is my _____ (type of relation i.e. sister).

I would like you to meet my _____ (type of

relation i.e. colleague), _____ (name of person

being introduced).

How did you two meet?

We met in/at/on _____ (location i.e. school,

college, vacation, work).

How long have you known each other?

We have known each other for _____ (number

of days/weeks/months/years)

days/weeks/months/years.

We are very close to each other.

We are not close.

I (do not) know them very well.

-After reviewing the common terms for other people and sentence formats, ask your student to describe some people that they know and how they are related to one another or how they met. Make sure to ask if these kind of questions are okay with your student. If they do not wish to divulge such personal information (i.e. who they live with or how they met their spouse), let them know they can make the answers up. It is the speaking practice that counts here, along with the understanding of what title means what.
-Role-play with one another by asking each other questions about people in your lives. Again, this too can be fictional or real information. If the student is okay with sharing their real information about the people in their lives, this will be great practice for them, as people often ask about family when first conversing with a stranger.

-Ask them if there is a specific relation which has not been covered that they would like to know the name for; this can be anything from a 3rd cousin removed to another distant relative.

-Assign the suggested homework and be prepared to check it during your next tutoring session.

Homework: Conversation about People

Answer the following questions to the best of your ability.
Write out all of your answers in full sentences and make sure they are grammatically correct.
Give this to your tutor during your next tutoring session for corrections.
Your answers can be real or fictional.

1. Who do you live with?

2. How long have you know your best friend?

3. How did you meet your significant other

(spouse/boyfriend/girlfriend)?

4. How long have you and your significant other

known each other?

5. Which family member are you closest with?

6. Are you close with your colleagues/classmates?

7. How long have you known your closest

colleague/classmate?

8. How did you first meet your closest colleague/classmate?

9. How many sisters do you have?

10. How many brothers do you have?

ESL Lesson Plan 17: Possessive Pronouns

Description: In this lesson, your student will learn or review possessive pronouns. These pronouns are important for expressing belonging. The student will have the opportunity to read, write, listen to and say these pronouns.

Lesson Guide:

-Create a list of possessive pronouns for the student. Even if they are already familiar with most of the pronouns, it is good to have it in front of them during a review.

Possessive Pronoun List Example:

I: my, mine
You: your, yours
He: his
She: her, hers
It: its
Them: their, theirs
Whose

-Many times, there is confusion over how to use the "whose" question word. Explain to the student that "whose" implies possession and that this is the question word they should use when asking about possession.

-Explain to the student that pronouns take the place of the actual nouns. Nouns can also be possessive. (i.e. Sara's bike; people's choice)
-Have the student create sentences and questions with the possessive pronouns out loud. Make sure they understand how to use and pronounce each one correctly. You can also create sentences and have them read them out loud.

Examples of Sentences with Possessive Pronouns:

My cup has coffee in it.

Your chair is broken.

His leg fell asleep during class.

Her luggage could not be found anywhere.

Its leg was completely healed after only three days.

Their flight arrived right on schedule.

Whose pen is this?

Is this **your** pen?

Where is **his** jacket?

-Practice creating and saying possessive pronoun sentences out loud with your student. Allow them to

get comfortable with these pronouns through repetition.
-Assign the suggested homework and be prepared to correct it during your next tutoring session.

Homework: Possessive Pronouns

Fill in the correct possessive pronoun.
The pronouns in parentheses are hints.

1. (She) _____ blender was broken and

she needed to buy a new one.

2. (He) _____ jacket wasn't where he last

put it.

3. (I) _____ cats like to sleep all day and

play all night.

4. (They) _____ child was one of the top

students in the entire class.

5. (It) _____ paws were painted white

after the dog stepped in wet paint by accident.

6. (Who) _____ red car is that in the

parking lot?

7. That dress is (I) _____.

8. Once Peter saw the big screen TV at the store, he wanted it to be (he) _____.

9. Kelly thought the company car was all (she) _____ for the weekend, but she actually needed to share it with her coworker.

10. Jonathan found (he) _____ keys after looking for them for over an hour.

11. (She) _____ patience had run out after babysitting a two-year-old the entire weekend.

12. Mary brought a batch of (she) _____ homemade cookies to work.

13. Jessie had not realized (she) _____ laptop was missing until she needed to check her email.

14. (I) _____ computer runs really well when I don't have multiple websites open at once.

15. (I) _____ dog likes to go on walks in the afternoon.

16. (We) _____ grandson visits us every Sunday.

17. Peter likes (he) _____ coffee black with two sugars.

18. Cynthia can't find (she) _____ notebook anywhere.

19. If you browse (she) _____ ipod, you will find many jazz and pop songs.

20. (We) _____ favorite type of family vacation is one where we can stay at home all day and relax.

ESL Lesson Plan 18: Your and You're

Description: As social media is becoming more and more popular, it is also becoming more evident that even native English speakers have a very difficult time remembering which "your" to use. Let your student be ahead of the pack by devoting a tutoring session to this often-confused grammatical choice. By showing him or her the proper usage for each term early on, they will be less likely to make this mistake in the future.

Lesson Guide:

-Write down both "your" and "you're" for your student. Ask them to pronounce each of them. They will quickly learn these two terms are pronounced exactly the same (which might be why many often confuse their spelling).
-Explain to the student the exact meaning of each term. They will see these terms are not interchangeable and will learn how to use them properly from the beginning.

Example Explanations of "Your" and "You're":

Your is possessive and signifies possession. You would only use **your** when showing this possession. For example: **your** coat, **your** notebook – but **NEVER** you're coat, you're notebook, etc.

You're is a contraction of **you are. You are** is a conjugation of the verb **to be** for the word **you**. Although **you're** sounds exactly like **your** in speech, it should never be spelled as such. For English professors and people with a good grasp of the English language, confusing these two terms is like running fingernails down a chalkboard. Okay - maybe not that drastic – but pretty close!

-Write out sentences with the student using both terms. This exercise focuses on repetition, but you can get some pronunciation practice here, too.

Example Sentences with Your:

Your jacket is unzipped.

Did you get **your** luggage yet?

This is **your** sweater.

Will you bring **your** laptop with you to my party?

Your baby is adorable!

Example Sentences with You're:

You're scheduled for a nine o'clock meeting

tomorrow.

You're welcome back anytime!

You're dress has been tailored by the tailor shop

and is ready to be picked up.

You're so beautiful when you smile.

You're on the student roster twice.

-Have the student read off each of the sentences, or create unique ones with your student.
-You can also leave out the "your" or "you're" when constructing the sentences, and have your student fill in the correct form. After that, they can read the sentences to you.
-Assign the suggested homework and be prepared to correct it during your next tutoring session.

Homework: Your and You're

Fill in the correct term (**your** or **you're**) for each sentence.

1. _____ mother asked me to give you

_____ jacket while _____

outside.

2. John borrowed _____ pen, but he

said he would give it right back in a few

minutes.

3. _____ blushing! Are you

embarrassed by the announcement made about

you?

4. Since _____ early, _____

seat can be closer to the speaker when the

seminar begins.

5. _____ dog has been barking for over an hour now.

6. If _____ planning to come with us to the mountains, make sure to bring _____ own gear.

7. _____ living room looks amazing with all of the new furniture!

8. Did you buy _____ tickets to Mexico yet? I still haven't reserved mine.

9. _____ taxi is here. Call me when _____ at your house.

10. _____ scheduled to arrive in Los Angeles at 3 in the afternoon.

11. I love that dress on you, _____ so extravagant in it!

12. Don't worry, _____ not late. That clock on the wall is not working.

13. You left _____ purse at the movie theater last night. We retrieved it from the lost and found.

14. _____ staying in room 146. Check out is at noon tomorrow. Enjoy your stay here!

15. If _____ planning on bringing your pets to a hotel, make sure they have a pet-friendly policy first.

16. Mary, _____ restaurant reservations have been cancelled by someone in _____ party.

17. _____ cats are very fun to watch, they are so active and playful!

18. _____ food is ready and will be

brought out to you shortly.

19. If _____ interested in buying a

second home, make sure _____

mortgage payments on your first home are up-

to-date.

20. Did you leave _____ keys in my
car?

ESL Lesson Plan 19: Frequency Adverbs

Description: Frequency adverbs are commonly used in both writing and speech. Your student has probably heard a few themselves without knowing what they are called. Frequency adverbs are useful for showing how often or how seldom an action is performed. In this lesson, your student will get acquainted with the most common frequency adverbs.

Lesson Guide:

-Make a list of the most used frequency adverbs and show it to your student.
-Have them read the words back to you after you have shown them how to pronounce each term.
-Listen for proper pronunciation.

Example List of Frequency Adverbs:

Always
Frequently
Usually
Normally
Often
Sometimes
Occasionally
Seldom
Rarely
Never

-With always signifying the most frequency and never signifying the least, make sure your student understands how to use the terms according to their definitions of frequency.

-Make sentences with different frequency adverbs that show proper usage of each term.

-Have your student create and say sentences with frequency adverbs. Listen for errors and congratulate them if there are none.

-Assign the suggested homework and be prepared to correct it during your next tutoring session.

Homework: Frequency Adverbs

Write a short story that includes all of the frequency adverbs you learned during your lesson. The story can be between 300-500 words. Make sure to show you English tutor your story during your next tutoring session. They will be able to correct not only your frequency adverb usage, but also your grammar.

ESL Lesson Plan 20: Ways to Say Goodbye

Description: There are many ways of saying goodbye in English. The most appropriate approach depends on the person you are talking to, the situation and your knowledge level of parting words. In this lesson, the student will learn how to part ways on the phone, with strangers, with colleagues, with family or friends and more.

Lesson Guide:

-Ask your student which parting words they already know. Write them down.
-Introduce your student to more ways of saying goodbye.
-Break down the various ways of parting into appropriate categories, so that your student understands how and when to use them.
-Make sure to mention which phrases are formal or informal.
-Practice pronunciation and enunciation with your student.

Example Ways of Saying Goodbye:

Formal:

"Have a great evening. See you tomorrow!"

"Talk to you later."

"Take care."

"Take it easy."

"Bye!"

"So long!"

Informal:

"Later."

"Peace out." (slang)

"Catch you later."

-Mention to your student which parting words are okay to use formally on the phone or in person with clients, customer service, or acquaintances.

-The student should understand the limitations of informal ways for saying goodbye. Let them know which age groups typically use the slang terminology and who they say it to. Your student should know that slang is informal and normally used by younger people.

-Assign the suggested homework and remember to ask about it during your next tutoring session.

Homework: Ways to Say Goodbye

Pay attention to all of the different ways people say goodbye to each other in movies, in person, on the radio, in writing via conversations on the internet/social media and on the telephone.
Write down any new terms you have not learned yet. Show them to your English tutor during your next tutoring session.
You might be surprised at the dozens of ways to say goodbye!

Conclusion

This concludes our one-on-one English as a second language lesson plans. Check major retailers for additional ESL guides from Inspired By English. English is a living, breathing language that is constantly changing with each generation.

The idioms or phrasal verbs that were popular for one decade might be phased out during the next decade. As an English tutor, you have the unique position to teach your students real English that they can utilize in their everyday lives.

Often times, you will be the only one that your student feels comfortable enough to speak English with, and that's okay during the beginning. Encourage your students to venture out of their comfortable and to engage in conversation with other native English speakers. During your tutoring sessions with them, they should get ample speaking time.

Thanks for choosing Inspired By English as your source for one-on-one ESL lesson plans for beginner students.

BONUS:

If you enjoyed this guide, please leave feedback and receive a free English ebook as a thank you.

How to receive your free bonus ebook:

1. Write a review on the website this ebook was purchased
2. Email esltutor@inspiredbyenglish.com with your username or link to where the review was written
3. Sit back and receive your free bonus by email.

InspiredByEnglish.com